D1518892

REASONS TO CARE ABOUT
GREAT APES
[Animals in Peril]

David Barker

Enslow Publishers, Inc.
40 Industrial Road
Box 398
Berkeley Heights, NJ 07922
USA
http://www.enslow.com

Library of Congress Cataloguing-in-Publication Data
Barker, David, 1959-
  Top 50 reasons to care about great apes : animals in peril / by David Barker.
    p. cm. — (Top 50 reasons to care about endangered animals)
  Includes bibliographical references and index.
  Summary: "Readers will learn about the great apes—their life cycle, habitats, young, and why these animals are endangered"—Provided by publisher.
  ISBN 978-0-7660-3456-3
  1. Apes—Juvenile literature. 2. Endangered species—Juvenile literature. I. Title. II. Title: Top fifty reasons to care about great apes.
  QL737.P96B346 2010
  599.88—dc22
                              2008048691

Printed in the United States of America

092009 Lake Book Manufacturing, Inc., Melrose Park, IL

10 9 8 7 6 5 4 3 2 1

To Our Readers: We have done our best to make sure all Internet Addresses in this book were active and appropriate when we went to press. However, the author and the publisher have no control over and assume no liability for the material available on those Internet sites or on other Web sites they may link to. Any comments or suggestions can be sent by e-mail to comments@enslow.com or to the address on the back cover.

Enslow Publishers, Inc., is committed to printing our books on recycled paper. The paper in every book contains 10% and 30% post-consumer waste (PCW). The cover board on the outside of each book contains 100% PCW. Our goal is to do our part to help young people and the environment too!

Photographs: Jan Rysavy/iStockphoto, cover inset, 1; George Clerk/iStockphoto, 1; Anup Shah/Nature Picture Library, 4, 16, 18, 22, 23, 24, 57, 84; Karl Ammann/Nature Picture Library, 6, 13, 27, 42, 51, 55, 56, 64, 95; Steven Tilston/iStockphoto, 9; iStockphoto, 10, 48, 74; Red Line Editorial, 14; Bruce Davidson/Nature Picture Library, 17, 28, 39; Jeryl Tan/iStockphoto, 21; Ingo Arndt/Nature Picture Library, 29; Jurie Maree/iStockphoto, 30; Jean-Marc Bouju/AP Images, 31; Uwe Lein/AP Images, 32; Christopher Courteau/Nature Picture Library, 35; Michael Krabs/Photolibrary, 36; Charles Taylor/iStockphoto, 40; Chris Pritchard/iStockphoto, 41; Charlie Neibergall/AP Images, 44; Imre Foeldi/AP Images, 47; Bettmann/Corbis, 52; Hanne & Jens Eriksen/Nature Picture Library, 58; Graeme Purdy/iStockphoto, 59; Jim Hudelson/AP Images, 60; Christine Eichin/iStockphoto, 62; AP Images, 67, 73, 86; Irwin Fedrainsyah/AP Images, 69; Juan Manuel Borrero/Nature Picture Library, 70; Jameson Weston/iStockphoto, 75; Chuck Babbitt/iStockphoto, 76; Georgette Douwma/Nature Picture Library, 79; Steve Helber/AP Images, 80; Themba Hadebe/AP Images, 83, 88; Jodi Jacobson/iStockphoto, 85; Nick Garbutt/Nature Picture Library, 91; Rodrique Ngowi/AP Images, 92; Eric Gevaert/iStockphoto, 94, 99; Martin Meissner/AP Images, 97

Cover caption: A mother orangutan carries her baby.
George Clerk/iStockphoto

CONTENTS

ENDANGERED GREAT APES

Many people confuse great apes with monkeys, but apes are not monkeys at all. You may know great apes as lovable clowns or as blood-thirsty monsters. But these are only the characters they have played in movies. In reality, great apes—which consist of two kinds of gorillas, two types of orangutans, chimpanzees, and bonobos—are neither clowns nor monsters. The truth is much more interesting, as scientists are discovering. The great apes are similar to humans in many ways yet unlike humans in many others. Each great ape is different from the others.

All six species of great apes are endangered today. They are included on the Red List of Endangered Species. This is a widely respected list of the world's endangered wildlife compiled by the International Union for Conservation of Nature (IUCN).

The great apes are threatened by hunting, loss of habitat, and disease. If these problems continue, great apes could become extinct.

However, all hope is not lost. The best way to help these animals is to learn about them and teach others about the dangers they face.

◀ THE GREAT APES ARE ENDANGERED.

GETTING TO KNOW GREAT APES

REASON TO CARE # 1

There Are Many Types of Great Apes

The great apes are made up of gorillas, chimpanzees, bonobos, and orangutans. These animals are grouped into species and subspecies.

There are two species of gorillas, the western gorilla and the eastern gorilla. All of these gorillas live in Africa. There are also two species of orangutans, the Bornean and the Sumatran. These species live in Asia. Gorillas and orangutans are also broken down into subspecies.

Currently, there is only one species of chimpanzee and one species of bonobo. But as scientists study these animals, they divide them into subspecies. For example, there are four subspecies of chimpanzees.

The great apes are all members of the family Hominidae, which means "human like." Humans are also members of the family Hominidae.

◀ THE EASTERN GORILLA WAS RECOGNIZED AS ITS OWN SPECIES IN 2001.

The Great Apes Are Primates

The great apes belong to the Primate order. There are more than 230 species of primates, but this number is changing as scientists reclassify the animals. Monkeys, lemurs, and gibbons are also primates.

Primates share many common characteristics. For example, most primates give birth to one offspring at a time. Unlike other animals that have four legs, primates usually have two arms and two legs. Primates have eyes on the fronts of their heads, which allows them to perceive depth. This means they can judge how far or how close an object is. They also have nails instead of claws, and each primate has a unique set of fingerprints.

► THE GREAT APES ARE PRIMATES, ALONG WITH MONKEYS, LEMURS, AND GIBBONS.

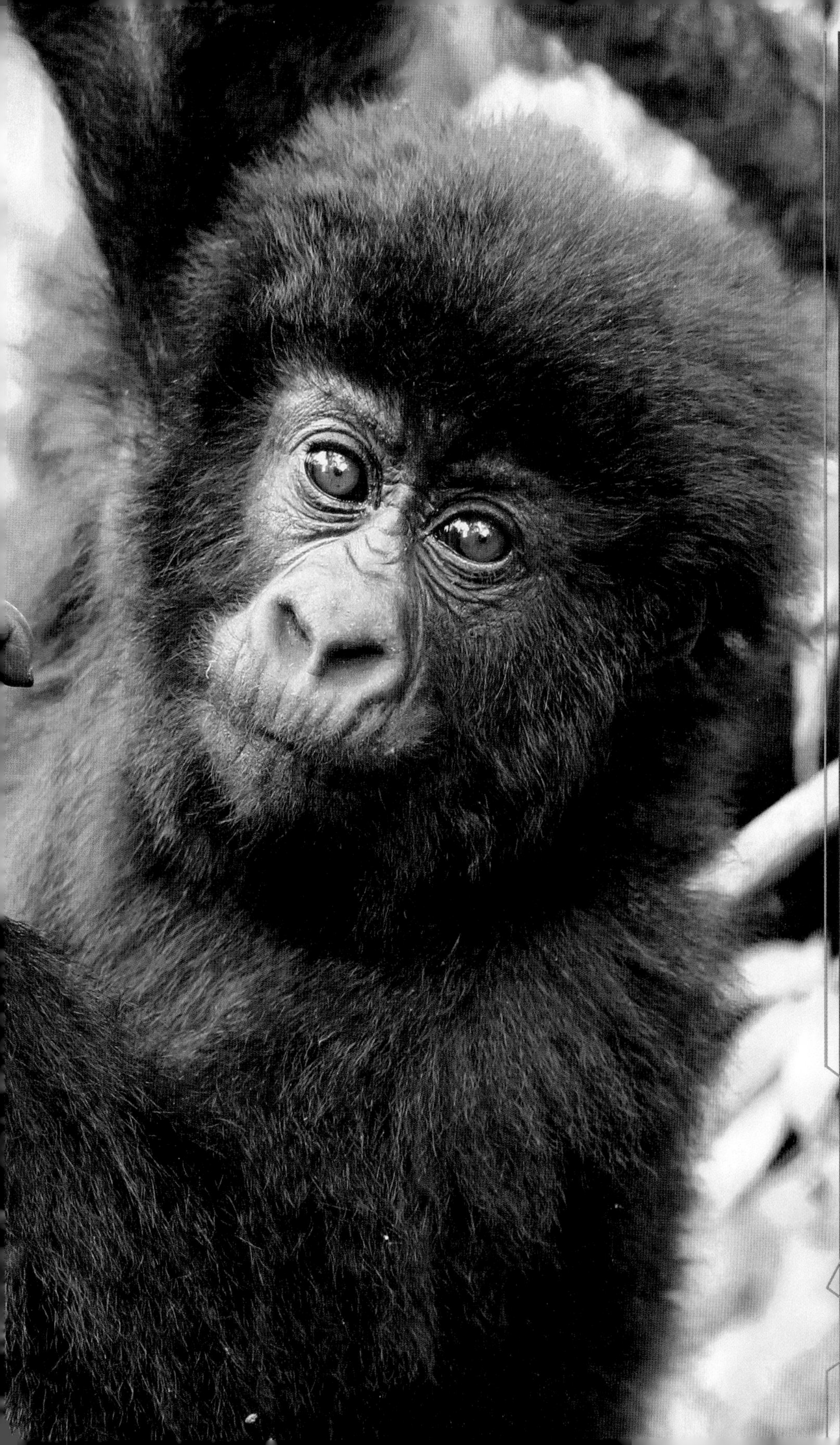

REASON TO CARE # 3

Great Apes Are Not Monkeys

It is common to hear people call an ape a monkey, but apes are different from monkeys. Both physical and mental differences set them apart.

For one, an ape does not have a tail. It has a flat chest, unlike a monkey, which has a dog-like chest. An ape also has a different type of shoulder joint that allows it to hang from its arms. So while a monkey walks along branches, an ape swings under them. The ape also has longer arms than legs, while a monkey's arms are shorter or the same length as its legs.

Apes are divided into two categories—great apes and lesser apes. Many species of gibbons make up the lesser apes.

◀ GREAT APES HAVE LONGER ARMS THAN LEGS.

Bonobos Are Not Chimpanzees

Bonobos were not identified as a species until 1929. Before that, they were thought to be chimpanzees. The bonobo was one of the last large mammals to be discovered by science.

While the two species do look very similar, scientists have identified differences in their appearances. A bonobo tends to be smaller than a chimpanzee. It also has characteristically narrow shoulders, a thin neck, and a smaller, rounder head. Its reddish lips stand out against a black face. With its high-pitched calls, a bonobo also sounds different than a chimpanzee.

The most telling differences between the two species are in behavior. Chimpanzees are always ready for a fight, while bonobos are much gentler. Bonobos are better thought of as lovers than fighters. Also, chimpanzee societies are male-centered, while female bonobos tend to dominate in their groups.

► BONOBOS ARE GENERALLY GENTLER THAN CHIMPANZEES.

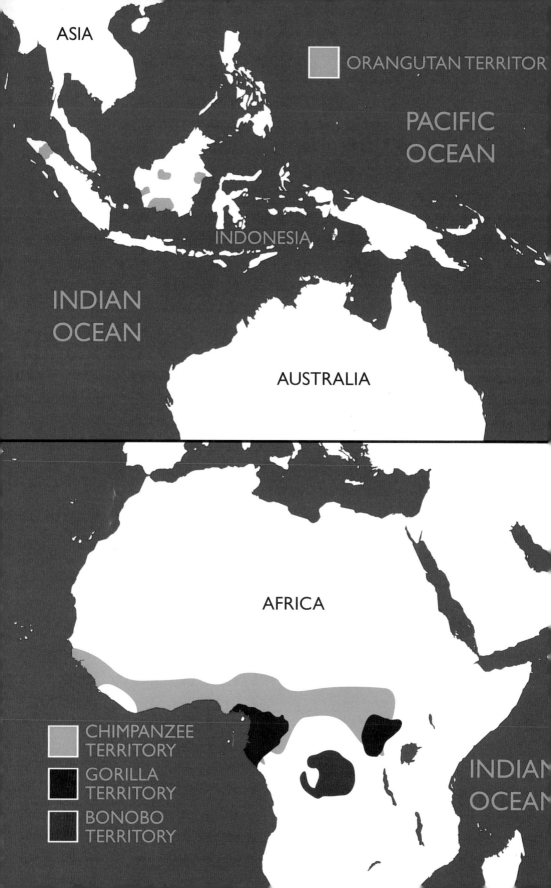

REASON TO CARE # 5

Great Apes Live Near the Equator

Most great apes live in tropical rain forests near the equator. Orangutans live on Indonesian islands in Southeast Asia. Gorillas, chimpanzees, and bonobos all live in Africa.

The Bornean orangutan is found only on the island of Borneo. The Sumatran orangutan is found only on the island of Sumatra. The word *orangutan* comes from Malay words meaning "person of the forest." The Malay are a native people of Sumatra.

Gorillas, which once made their homes across central Africa, are now found in two areas separated by 620 miles. The western gorilla is found in the west, and the eastern gorilla is found in the east.

Chimpanzees live in central Africa. They also live in Guinea and Sierra Leone in western Africa. Their habitats range from dense forested areas to open grasslands.

Bonobos are found in central Africa, south of the Congo River. The great apes dislike water and cannot swim. Western gorillas, chimpanzees, and bonobos cannot cross the wide Congo River.

◀ TOP: ORANGUTANS LIVE IN ASIA. BOTTOM: AFRICA IS HOME TO GORILLAS, CHIMPANZEES, AND BONOBOS.

Great Apes Live Long Lives

The great apes may live forty years or more in the wild. Many individuals never reach this age because infant deaths are common.

In captivity, great apes can live much longer because their needs are better known and therefore more easily met. Captive great apes also face fewer threats from humans. Apes in captivity can live to be more than fifty years old.

▼ PROTECTED GREAT APES CAN LIVE A LONG TIME, SUCH AS THIS OLDER CHIMPANZEE CARRYING A YOUNGER APE IN GOMBE NATIONAL PARK.

▲ THE LOSS OF FOREST HABITATS HURTS GREAT APES.

REASON TO CARE # 7

The Great Apes Are in Danger

Over the past fifty years, scientists have seen great apes' habitats and populations shrink quickly. Apes have fallen victim to hunting, the loss of forests, and disease.

Many organizations have formed to work on behalf of the great apes. Governments are beginning to take action too. Preventing the extinction of great apes will require preserving their forests and improving the lives of the people who live with them in Africa and Southeast Asia.

GREAT APES IN THE FOREST

REASON TO CARE # 8

Great Apes Are Built for Life in the Trees

As a primate, a great ape has certain traits that help it climb trees. It has an opposable thumb and big toe, which allow the ape to grasp objects with both its hands and feet. It has nails, too, rather than claws.

Great apes damage trees while they climb—but in a good way. The bent and broken branches make gaps in the forest canopy that allow sunlight to reach deeper into the floor of the forest. This sunlight nourishes plants that might have never grown without it.

◄ ORANGUTANS ARE EXPERT CLIMBERS.

Great Apes Eat Fruit

Great apes often climb trees to reach food. The animals eat shoots, leaves, and other plant parts, but they prefer to eat fruits. Where fruit is not as available, they depend on other foods.

The great apes know a lot about plants in their habitats. For example, an orangutan is able to recognize more than four hundred kinds of food plants. It also remembers where the plants are located and when they will be ripe. Although great apes enjoy plants, fruits, and seeds, some do eat meat. They may eat insects, such as ants and termites, as well as lizards and small mammals. Bonobos will eat a certain kind of caterpillar when it is available. Chimpanzees eat meat most frequently, with about 5 percent of their diet coming from meat.

▶ THE MAJORITY OF A GREAT APE'S DIET IS PLANT-BASED.

Chimpanzees Hunt in Groups

Unlike other great apes, male chimpanzees hunt in groups. They will capture, kill, and eat large mammals such as monkeys and forest antelopes.

Jane Goodall, a scientist who observed chimpanzees in Tanzania at Gombe National Park, saw that they cooperated as they hunted. The chimpanzees had more kills when they worked together to find prey.

▼ CHIMPANZEES SHARE A KILL.

▲ A CHIMPANZEE EATS SEED PODS IN TANZANIA.

REASON TO CARE # 11

Great Apes Help Spread Seeds

Great apes help plants by eating their fruits. A fruit contains a plant's seeds. When apes eat fruit, they carry the seeds in their digestive systems away from the parent plant. Then the apes leave the seeds on the forest floor in their droppings, which then act as fertilizer. This ensures that the new plants will be far away and will not fight for nutrients with the parent plant.

REASON TO CARE # 12

Orangutans Are Solitary Climbers

Unlike the other great apes, orangutans live mostly alone. Half of an orangutan's day is spent looking for food. The remaining time is spent at rest.

Orangutans live mostly in the trees where their food is found. In Sumatra, hungry tigers roam the forest floor. That also makes tree life a good choice for safety.

Orangutans have long arms and broad shoulders that help them climb. A fall from the trees can be deadly, however, so they are careful climbers. In the evening, an orangutan builds a nest in a tree and settles down to sleep.

[Orangutans have shaggy red hair, unlike the black hair of other great apes. They stand 4 to 5 feet (1.25 to 1.5 meters) tall. Adult males are about twice the size of females. They can weigh 175 to 300 pounds (80 to 135 kilograms), while females weigh 75 to 100 pounds (35 to 45 kilograms).]

◀ ORANGUTANS SPEND MUCH OF THEIR TIME CLIMBING IN TREES TO SEARCH FOR FOOD.

Bonobos Can Walk Upright

Bonobos prefer old forests with dense canopies and little undergrowth. They spend most of their day looking for food, often moving upright. Of all the great apes, bonobos seem the most adapted to walking on two legs. They move around their habitat looking for fruit and other plant parts in the trees and on the ground.

Bonobos, like other African great apes, sometimes eat whole leaves in the morning. A possible reason for this is to clean their bodies of parasites. The leaves pick up parasites in the ape's gut before passing out of the body.

The bonobo looks a lot like a chimpanzee, though it is somewhat lighter. Adult males weigh up to 100 pounds (45 kilograms), and females weigh 75 pounds (35 kilograms). They stand about 3 feet (1 meter) tall.

▶ BONOBOS OFTEN STAND UPRIGHT, SUCH AS THIS YOUNG BONOBO IN THE DEMOCRATIC REPUBLIC OF THE CONGO.

Gorillas Stay Close to the Ground

Gorillas live in forests with open canopies and lots of vegetation growing on the ground for them to eat. Adult gorillas rarely climb trees to find food, perhaps because they are the heaviest of the great apes. A gorilla walks on all fours, supporting its upper body on its knuckles. This is called knuckle-walking.

▼ KNUCKLE-WALKING ALLOWS A GORILLA TO MOVE EASILY ON THE GROUND.

▲ A GORILLA FAMILY RESTS TOGETHER IN RWANDA.

Gorillas live in family groups. A gorilla group eats in the morning and then rests for several hours. The young gorillas play, then all the gorillas nap. They feed again in the afternoon. In the evening, gorillas make nests on the ground or in trees.

A male gorilla weighs between 350 and 400 pounds (160 and 180 kilograms), while an adult female weighs between 165 and 200 pounds (75 and 90 kilograms). Gorillas stand 4 to 5.5 feet (1.25 to 1.75 meters) high.

Chimpanzees Are Good Climbers

Gorillas are not the only great ape species that knuckle-walks. Chimpanzees also walk on all fours, supporting the front of their bodies on their knuckles. But unlike gorillas, chimpanzees are also good climbers. They often have to climb trees to find food. They have long hands that help them hold onto branches and tree trunks.

▼ CHIMPANZEES HAVE LONG HANDS THAT HELP THEM CLIMB TREES.

▲ CHIMPANZEES WILL WALK ON TWO LEGS WHEN THEY ARE CARRYING SOMETHING.

Chimpanzees are usually uncomfortable walking on two legs. But sometimes chimpanzees walk upright if they are excited. They may stand on two legs to peer over tall grass or to use their hands to carry food.

Unlike orangutans and gorillas, male and female chimpanzees are similar in size. A male chimpanzee weighs about 95 pounds (43 kilograms), and a female weighs about 70 pounds (32 kilograms).

GREAT APE COMMUNITIES

REASON TO CARE # 16

Great Apes Usually Live in Groups

Except for the orangutan, great apes live in groups and are very social animals. They communicate with each other using gestures, facial expressions, touch, and voice. The groups are also organized, though the level of organization depends on the species. The groups have a dominant member (or members) that may be in charge of defending the group or sharing food. The leaders are male, except in the case of bonobos. These animals are remarkable for their female-run societies.

Female great apes are ready to leave their birth groups at six to ten years old. They will gradually join another group and will become mothers themselves at ten to fifteen years old, depending on the species. Male chimpanzees and bonobos stay in their birth groups for life, while male gorillas leave their birth group before age fifteen.

◀ GORILLAS AND OTHER GREAT APES COMMUNICATE THROUGH GESTURES, GRUNTS, AND TOUCH.

Male Chimpanzees Have Strong Rivalries

Chimpanzees are not only fierce predators, they can be fierce with each other as well. They are known to be competitive and aggressive within their loosely connected groups, which can include up to one hundred individuals.

Each chimpanzee group has a dominant male that is the group's leader. He shows his dominance through body language—standing upright and stamping his feet. Below the leader, males have varying levels of power according to their dominance rank. Dominant males do not stay in power for long, however. Males are often in a contest to become dominant. Competing males recruit other males to their side, resulting in strong male-male friendships. A fight between two chimpanzees will soon become a fight between two alliances of chimpanzees.

Different chimpanzee groups rarely get along. The groups fight to protect their territories. Male chimpanzees patrol and defend their territory from neighboring groups.

▶ A MALE CHIMPANZEE VOCALIZES IN A UGANDAN NATIONAL PARK.

REASON TO CARE # 18

Females Lead Bonobo Groups

Bonobos live in groups of about twenty. Females often dominate males in bonobo groups. This means the females are in control. These females eat first and receive the best choices of food. Mothers and sons are very close. A son's position in a group is supported by his mother. Strong female-female bonds form when a new female enters the group.

Bonobos are often less aggressive than chimpanzees, but they do fight. They will slap and kick each other, but they rarely bite like chimpanzees.

Unlike chimpanzee groups, bonobo groups are not in conflict by nature, though the bonobo groups are cautious when they first meet. At night, bonobo groups will come together, forming a large group that builds sleeping nests in trees.

◄ FEMALES OFTEN LEAD BONOBO GROUPS.

The Silverback Defends His Gorilla Group

Most gorillas travel in small family groups of usually fewer than ten individuals. Most of these groups have one adult male called the silverback, because the hair on a male gorilla's back turns silver when he matures. The silverback makes decisions for the group and defends the group from competing silverbacks. Each group also has several adult females and their offspring.

The gorilla is famous as the fierce King Kong in Hollywood movies. But despite its reputation, a gorilla rarely fights. The silverback will threaten other males to defend the group. He may beat his chest, charge toward his opponent, grunt, or roar loudly.

Gorilla groups avoid other groups and make noisy displays when they meet. But relationships between groups are not violent. Because of their generally peaceful nature, gorillas have earned the nickname gentle giants.

▶ SILVERBACK GORILLAS DEFEND AND MAKE DECISIONS FOR THEIR FAMILY GROUPS.

Orangutans Are Territorial

Orangutans are unusual among great apes because they live mostly alone. Males defend their territories from other males. Orangutan infants travel with their mothers until they are five or six years old. Females allow other females to be nearby and may be friendly to them. Adolescent female orangutans are more social and often travel in groups.

▼ TERRITORIAL MALE ORANGUTANS HAVE VERY SOLITARY BEHAVIOR PATTERNS.

▲ FEMALE ORANGUTANS WILL TOLERATE SOCIAL SETTINGS.

Young males wander alone for several years before they are strong enough to defend a territory from other males. The only time a male is not alone is when he is with a female with whom he has mated. When he is with a female, he will fight with other males to keep them away from her.

[An adult male orangutan makes a loud noise, known as a long call, to tell other orangutans that he is nearby. The long call challenges males while inviting females.]

REASON TO CARE # 21

Great Apes Groom
Each Other

All great apes groom, or clean, each other and may do so for hours at a time. An ape will pick through another ape's fur, removing dead skin, leaves, and bugs. Although orangutans live mostly alone, orangutan mothers still groom their young offspring.

Grooming is more than just about staying clean, however. Grooming can build bonds between the apes. This friendly, social activity often shows which apes are in charge. For example, female gorillas will groom each other, their young, and the silverback. The silverback, however, never grooms a female in return.

◄ BONOBOS FORM BONDS BY GROOMING EACH OTHER.

REASON TO CARE # 22

Humans Study Great Apes

The great apes have long fascinated humans. Early Europeans exploring Africa were amazed by the apes they found during their travels. English sailor Andrew Battell described a great ape he saw in Africa in 1625. He wrote, "This Pongo [ape] is in all proportions like a man; but that he is more like a giant in stature, than a man; for he is very tall, and hath a man's face, hollow-eyed, with long hair upon his brows."[1]

Scientists have studied apes for many years. Their findings reveal that the great apes are intelligent. Apes can use symbols and signs to express need. The Great Ape Trust in Iowa reports that this is strong evidence to show that apes understand a connection between words and objects.

◀ AN ORANGUTAN NAMED KNOBI SITS IN ITS PEN AT THE GREAT APE TRUST IN IOWA.

Great Apes Fit in the Theory of Evolution

Charles Darwin's theory of evolution is one way to explain the resemblance between apes and humans. Darwin believed that humans and apes are alike because they evolved from one ancestor species.

H. Lyn White Miles is a professor at the University of Tennessee. She has studied great ape language and behavior. In an essay on orangutans, she wrote, "There are significant differences between humans and great apes, but we share 98–99 percent of our genetic makeup with them."[2] The theory of evolution is one way scientists explain these similarities.

▶ SCIENTISTS BELIEVE THIS FOSSILIZED APE JAW BELONGED TO AN APE SPECIES THAT LIVED TEN MILLION YEARS AGO.

REASON TO CARE # 24
Great Apes Have Spindle Cells

Scientists who study apes have researched how apes feel emotions. Their studies have shown that apes have feelings similar to human emotions. Apes are able to feel these emotions because their brains are similar to human brains.

In 1925, scientist Constantin von Economo discovered spindle cells. These cells are in charge of social emotions, such as love, anger, and feeling connected. Apes have spindle cells, which allow them to feel these emotions. Apes form bonds with family members. They demonstrate anger when something upsets them.

Until recently, scientists believed that only humans and apes had spindle cells. But recent studies of other animals have shown that spindle cells are present in the brains of some whales as well.

◄ SPINDLE CELLS IN APES ALLOW THEM TO EXPRESS SOCIAL EMOTIONS, SUCH AS LOVE.

Great Apes Can Solve Problems

Intelligence is difficult to describe and measure. Scientists measure animals' intelligence by comparing animal behavior to human behavior. The great apes are excellent problem-solvers. They are able to open complicated latches and use some tools.

Great apes can trick each other (and humans) to get something they want. This shows they can see the world from another individual's point of view. This ability also allows great apes to help each other. In the book *Bonobo: The Forgotten Ape*, caretaker Barbara Bell described an example of bonobos helping each other. Kidogo was a sick bonobo in the Milwaukee County Zoo in Wisconsin. Kidogo could not understand zookeepers' requests. Other bonobos that understood what the keepers were asking helped Kidogo. The bonobos took Kidogo's hand and helped him move where he needed to go.

▶ SOME CHIMPANZEES ARE ABLE TO FIGURE OUT HOW LOCKS AND KEYS WORK.

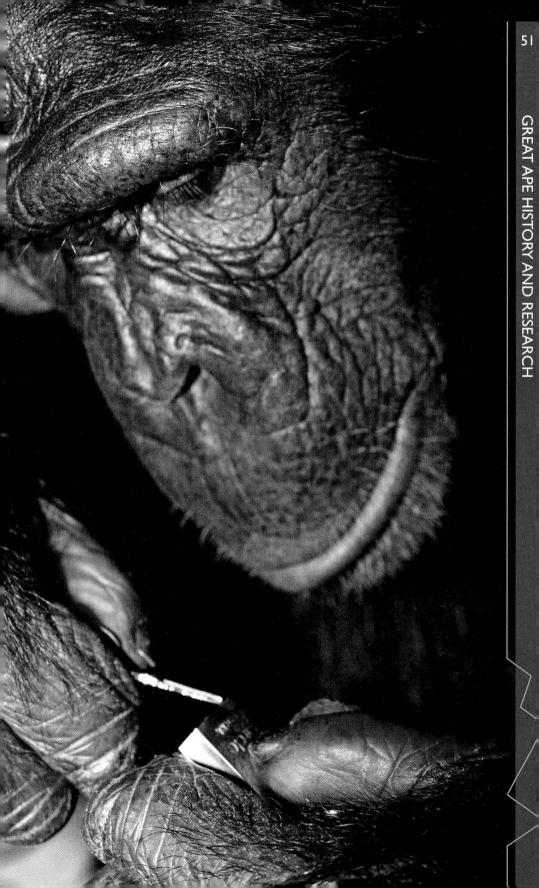

REASON TO CARE # 26

Great Apes Can Learn Sign Language

Scientists have tried to teach language to great apes. Whether the apes have truly learned to use language is not accepted by everyone, but many believe that is the case. Some apes have learned American Sign Language, the language used by deaf people. Dr. Francine Patterson worked with Koko, a gorilla, to teach it to use sign language. Patterson is the president and research director of the Gorilla Foundation/Koko.org. She has spent many years working with and writing about gorillas.

Other great apes, such as Kanzi, a bonobo, communicate through symbols on special boards or computers. Some of these animals are able to make simple sentences by combining words they have never seen together. These sentences describe something that the apes want.

◄ DR. FRANCINE PATTERSON TAUGHT SIGN LANGUAGE TO KOKO, A GORILLA.

Great Apes Make and Use Tools

Making a tool is one step beyond using something that is just lying around. Chimpanzees use a variety of tools in the wild. They use two stones to crack nuts. They strip leaves from branches, making thin sticks to fish for termites in termite mounds. And they repair the end when it becomes ragged.

The other great apes rarely use tools in the wild because they do not need them. However, all of these animals can be expert tool users when they live around humans. Also, great apes are not born knowing how to use a tool. They must watch others using it and practice themselves.

▶ A YOUNG CHIMPANZEE USES A GRASS STEM TO FISH FOR TERMITES.

Great Apes Communicate Feelings

Great apes have many emotions and communicate those feelings to others. However, the way they express their feelings is often different. Some scientists have studied the way apes express emotions. They try to interpret the apes' facial expressions.

▼ SOME SCIENTISTS INTERPRET FACIAL EXPRESSIONS SUCH AS THIS BONOBO'S AS EITHER HAPPINESS OR AGGRESSION.

▲ THE GREAT APES CAN COMMUNICATE EMOTION TO EACH OTHER THROUGH FACIAL EXPRESSION.

When great apes play together, they hold their mouths open with their lips relaxed, partially covering their teeth. This is their play expression. They also make hoarse breathing sounds that might be laughter.

Disappointed great apes hold their lips in a pouting expression. This might happen when another ape will not hand over a piece of food. A grin normally means a chimpanzee or bonobo is afraid of something. But these apes also grin when they are happy.

Great Apes Are Caring Parents

Newborn great apes are helpless and cling to their mothers for six months or longer in some species. They depend on their mothers for several years as they slowly become independent. The childhood of a great ape is long compared with other primates. For example, gorilla infants begin to make and sleep in their own nests at two years old. Chimpanzees may do so at five.

▼ A BORNEAN ORANGUTAN MOTHER AND BABY

▲ A BABY GORILLA RIDES ON ITS MOTHER'S BACK.

In gorilla, chimpanzee, and bonobo communities, a birth is a fairly rare event. All of the members of the group are interested in the newborn, wanting to touch it and hold it. They help look after and play with the infant. Even the silverback—the male leader in a group of gorillas—will play with young gorillas.

	Length of pregnancy	Weight of newborn
Gorillas	8–9.5 months	3–5 pounds (1.4–2.3 kilograms)
Chimpanzees	7–8 months	3–4 pounds (1.4–1.8 kilograms)
Bonobos	8 months	2.5–3 pounds (1.1–1.4 kilograms)
Orangutans	7.5–8.5 months	3.5–4.5 pounds (1.6–2 kilograms)

REASON TO CARE # 30

Great Apes Have Assisted in Medical Research

Because chimpanzees and bonobos share so many genetic similarities with humans, they have been used for medical and psychological research. Studies that relied on these apes helped scientists make medical advances for people, but many people believed the methods were inhumane.

Apes are currently used very rarely for research. In 1975, the United States adopted an agreement that said it would stop importing wild chimpanzees for research. In 2005, a private facility in Louisiana—Chimp Haven—began receiving chimpanzees retired from research.

[Scientists believe that the HIV virus, which causes AIDS in humans, developed from a virus found in chimpanzees.]

◄ CHIMP HAVEN PROVIDES A HOME FOR CHIMPANZEES THAT HAVE BEEN RETIRED FROM RESEARCH.

GREAT APES IN CULTURE

REASON TO CARE # 31

Early Explorers Encountered Great Apes

The peoples of central Africa have always lived with gorillas, chimpanzees, and bonobos. The first description of a great ape to Europeans was in 470 B.C. by the explorer Hanno, who came from the Middle East. He brought the African word *gorilla* to Europe, saying he had seen many "savages . . . whose bodies were covered with hair, and which our interpreter called gorillas."[3] African apes were next described in 1625 and in many writings afterward.

The Dayak peoples of the island of Borneo lived with orangutans, calling an orangutan a forest person. Some Dayaks believed orangutans were ghosts that could disappear when they wanted. The Dutchman Jacob Bontius first described orangutans to Europeans in 1658.

◀ THE GORILLA WAS FIRST NAMED BY AFRICANS.

REASON TO CARE # 32

Jane Goodall Studied Chimpanzees in Tanzania

Jane Goodall was born in England in 1934. In 1960, Goodall began to study chimpanzees in Gombe National Park in Tanzania.

Goodall had daily contact with the chimpanzees. By observing them, she found that the chimpanzees used tools. They would use reeds, branches, and roots around them to catch termites to eat.

Goodall also made another startling discovery. She found that chimpanzees ate meat. Previously, scientists had believed that chimpanzees ate mainly fruits, leaves, and insects. But Goodall observed the chimpanzees eating the meat of small animals, such as rodents.

Goodall has written books about her findings. She has even made movies about the chimpanzees at the Gombe National Park.

◀ JANE GOODALL HAS SPENT MANY YEARS STUDYING CHIMPANZEES IN TANZANIA.

Dian Fossey Spent Many Years Studying Gorillas

Human knowledge of the great apes grew rapidly when scientists began research studies in the 1960s. These projects lasted many years.

Dian Fossey was one researcher who spent a great deal of time studying apes. She specifically studied mountain gorillas in Africa. She first visited Africa in 1963 and returned in 1966 to begin a long-term study of gorillas. By spending time with the animals, she was able to gain their trust. This allowed her to observe them closely.

Fossey continued to study and write about mountain gorillas for the rest of her life. Her studies were published in *National Geographic* magazine. She learned much about their behavior. Her life ended abruptly in 1985 when she was murdered in her cabin in Africa.

[Dian Fossey learned to copy gorilla noises. Whenever she approached, she calmed the gorillas by making the contented noises the animals make during their midday nap.]

▶ DIAN FOSSEY STUDIED MOUNTAIN GORILLAS IN AFRICA.

Biruté Galdikas Works to Save Orangutans

Biruté Galdikas has spent much of her life studying orangutans. Since 1971, Galdikas has specifically studied the orangutans living on the island of Borneo.

Through observation, Galdikas learned how orangutans solve problems. She also studied how orangutans interact, communicate, and reproduce.

Gladikas noted that satellite photos taken between 1982 and 1990 showed about one third of Sumatra's forests were destroyed. By raising awareness of habitat conditions, Galdikas has continued to help orangutans survive in the wild and to preserve their natural environment.

[Jane Goodall, Dian Fossey, and Biruté Galdikas were all taught and encouraged by Louis Leakey, the scientist who discovered many human ancestor fossils in Africa. These scientists and many others have helped humans better understand the great apes.]

▶ BIRUTÉ GALDIKAS CARRIES AN ORANGUTAN NAMED ISABEL IN BORNEO.

REASON TO CARE # 35

Several Great Apes Have Been Famous

Chimpanzees have often appeared in Hollywood movies. The character Tarzan was always accompanied by a chimpanzee. During the 1930s and 1940s, a chimpanzee called Cheeta played the role of Tarzan's sidekick.

Snowflake was an albino (white) western gorilla that was captured in 1966 or 1967. Snowflake lived at a zoo in Barcelona, Spain, until he died in 2003. Snowflake was featured in a story in *National Geographic* that made the public aware of the threats to gorillas.

◄ VISITORS CAME FROM ALL OVER THE WORLD TO SEE SNOWFLAKE, AN ALBINO GORILLA.

Chimpanzees Have
Been Astronauts

HAM and Enos were chimpanzees that flew into space as part of the Mercury program of the early 1960s. HAM was born in Cameroon. He was named after the lab that prepared him for his space mission: the Holloman Aerospace Medical Center in New Mexico.

On January 31, 1961, HAM became the first chimpanzee in space. His flight did not orbit Earth, but it reached an altitude of 157 miles. During the flight, HAM aptly performed the tasks he was trained for. HAM's flight was followed by a similar mission with the first American astronaut Alan Shepard. Afterward, HAM lived in zoos from 1963 until he died in 1983.

Enos came from a wildlife park in Florida. After training, Enos entered orbit on November 29, 1961. He orbited Earth twice before splashing down. Enos's flight was followed three months later by a similar flight by astronaut John Glenn. Enos died from a disease only eleven months after his mission.

► HAM ON THE DECK OF A RESCUE SHIP AFTER HIS MISSION IN 1961

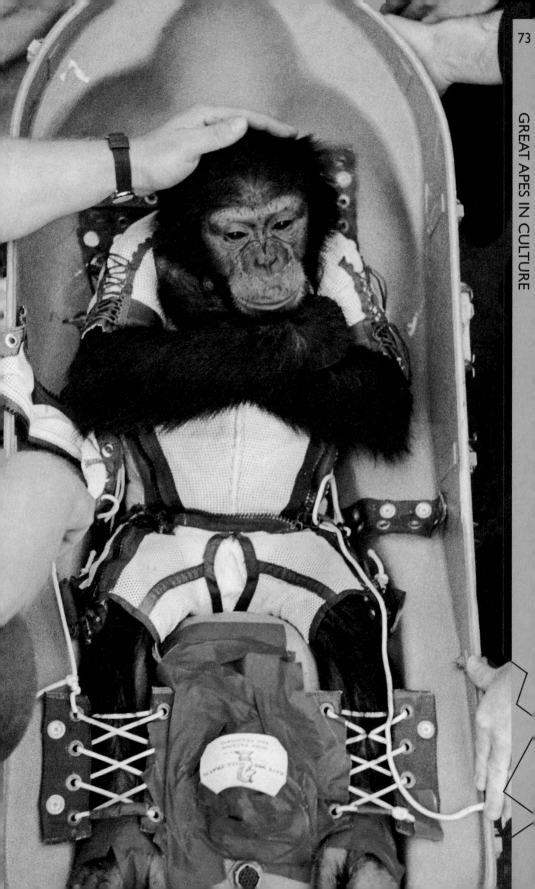

Thousands of Great Apes Live in Zoos

Probably thousands of great apes around the world live in zoos. Most of them were also born in zoos. In 1975, countries around the world signed the Convention on International Trade of Endangered Species (CITES) treaty. This made it illegal in many places to capture wild great apes for zoos.

▼ BONOBOS REST IN THEIR ZOO HABITAT.

▲ ORANGUTANS IN ZOOS NEED LOTS OF TREES FOR CLIMBING.

Some people and organizations do not believe zoos should keep great apes. They argue that the apes would be better off in the wild. Zoos argue that the great apes in captivity help educate people about the threats to great apes in the wild. Many zoos have educational programs for students and the public. Zoos also provide many scientists the opportunity to study the animals.

REASON TO CARE # 38

The Great Apes'
Situation Isn't Funny

Great apes might look cute or funny on TV or in the movies, but the truth is they need our help more than our laughter. Some scientists argue that portraying chimpanzees as comical characters makes people think of them as not endangered.

A study was carried out by the Lincoln Park Zoo in Chicago and was published in the journal *Science* in March 2008. In the study, nearly one thousand people were asked about their attitudes toward apes. The study showed that people did not recognize that great apes are endangered because apes are often shown on TV, movies, and advertisements. The lead author, Steve Ross, said, "The inappropriate portrayal of great apes in advertisements undermines the scientific, welfare, and conservation goals that we . . . work hard to achieve."[4]

◀ THE GREAT APES ARE ENDANGERED AND NEED OUR HELP TO SURVIVE.

Great Apes Are Losing Their Forest Habitats

Logging is the business of cutting down trees for wood. Illegal logging is responsible for most of the deforestation in Sumatra and Borneo, the islands in Indonesia and Malaysia where orangutans live. Illegal logging even occurs in the wildlife parks, which once were the safe haven of these great apes. In Indonesia and Malaysia, forests are being cut down to make room for palm oil plantations.

Both illegal and legal deforestation destroys ape habitats and also makes the apes more vulnerable to hunters, because sparse forests make the apes more visible. A 2007 report published by the United Nations Environment Programme warned: "If the immediate crisis in securing the future survival of the orangutan and the protection of national parks is not resolved, very few wild orangutans will be left within two decades."[5]

► BECAUSE OF INDUSTRIES SUCH AS LOGGING, GREAT APES ARE LOSING THE FORESTS THEY RELY ON.

REASON TO CARE # 40
Poaching Threatens Great Apes

Poachers are people who illegally kill or steal wild animals, especially endangered and protected animals. Great apes are poached for trophies, meat, and for capture. Some hunters take the apes alive to sell them. But many poachers kill apes, especially gorillas, because apes' body parts are sought after. Some poachers collect gorilla skulls, hands, feet, and skins.

In addition to poachers, the World Wildlife Fund (WWF) reports that some tribal groups in Western and Central Africa use ape body parts for traditional medicines. Although these practices are decreasing, much harm has been done to great ape populations by killing them for body parts.

◀ SOME POACHERS KILL GORILLAS TO COLLECT THEIR SKULLS.

Wars Threaten Great Apes

In war-torn countries, hunting for bushmeat is also a serious threat to great apes. International and national laws are in place to protect great apes from hunters. However, the laws are often not enforced. During times of war or famine when food is scarce, villagers and local people turn to killing animals for meat. In such conditions, there are too few wildlife officers, and those officers in place risk being killed by hunters or soldiers.

In the Democratic Republic of the Congo, many bonobos live in a war zone. Sometimes, these bonobos have been killed for food. About six thousand gorillas across Africa are also killed for bushmeat each year.

[Many local peoples have a taboo against killing bonobos, which means they believe that it is wrong. The Mongandu tribe in Africa believes that a bonobo once helped a tribe member who was stuck in a tree. After that, the tribe believed it was wrong to kill any bonobos in the forest.]

▶ A RANGER AT VIRUNGA NATIONAL PARK IN RUTSHURU, CONGO, OBSERVES THE GRAVES OF SIX MOUNTAIN GORILLAS THAT WERE KILLED DURING WARFARE THERE.

Great Apes Are
Captured as Pets

Very few orangutans are hunted for meat. The main reason people hunt orangutans is to capture their young. They sell the young as pets and to zoos for profit. In most cases, the mother is killed during the infant's capture.

▼ A RESCUED BABY ORANGUTAN IN SUMATRA, INDONESIA

▲ BABY ORANGUTANS AT A REHABILITATION CENTER IN BORNEO

Orangutans are protected by international law, Indonesian law, and Malaysian law. But many people in these countries do not consider the crime of taking an orangutan from the forest seriously, so the laws are not always enforced. In 2006, about one thousand orangutans were rescued from smugglers and placed in rehabilitation centers.

REASON TO CARE # 43

Great Apes Catch Human Diseases

Chimpanzees and gorillas share a habitat in Africa. Although these apes are threatened by hunting and deforestation, in some locations where chimpanzees come in contact with humans, disease is the main cause of death.

Chimpanzees catch many human diseases, including the deadly Ebola virus. In 2003, an outbreak of the Ebola virus in the Democratic Republic of the Congo killed 114 people. It also possibly took the lives of eight hundred gorillas in the Lossi Gorilla Sanctuary. Declines of gorillas and chimpanzees are measured by observing and counting the number of empty sleeping nests. In some areas, populations are thought to decline by 50 to 90 percent following Ebola epidemics.

◄ HERCULES, A GORILLA THAT LIVED IN THE DALLAS ZOO, DIED IN 2008 AFTER A PROCEDURE FOR SPINAL DISEASE.

GREAT APE CONSERVATION

REASON TO CARE # 44

Conservationists Unite to Help Great Apes

In 2005, a meeting was held in the Democratic Republic of the Congo. People came from countries where great apes live. These people discussed threats to great apes, such as deforestation, poaching, and the illegal wildlife trade. Some rebel armies in parts of Africa had killed gorillas living nearby.

All of these threats worried scientists, who believed that great ape populations were dwindling. At the end of the conference, the members agreed to control poaching. They also agreed to help local residents learn to live in harmony with the great apes and other animals living around them.

◄ PARK RANGERS IN THE DEMOCRATIC REPUBLIC OF THE CONGO WORK TO PROTECT GREAT APES AND OTHER ENDANGERED ANIMALS.

Laws Protect Orangutans

Orangutans are protected by international laws. Laws also exist in Indonesia and Malaysia, where they live. Because they are protected by the Convention on International Trade of Endangered Species (CITES), orangutans may not be moved across international borders. In Indonesia, it is illegal to hunt or disturb an orangutan. In Malaysia, orangutans cannot be hunted or captured. These countries also have created parks to protect the habitat of orangutans.

In December 2008, scientists on the Indonesian island of Borneo made an amazing discovery. They found a previously unknown population of orangutans that could be as large as two thousand. The find demonstrated to conservationists that preserving habitats and enforcing laws can help save great ape species.

▶ WORKERS CARE FOR ORANGUTANS AT A REHABILITATION CENTER IN BORNEO.

REASON TO CARE # 46

Conservation Funds
Help Great Apes

In 2000, U.S. Congress passed the Great Ape Conservation Act. The growing threats to great apes spurred lawmakers to pass this bill, which created the Great Ape Conservation Fund. This law is modeled after similar conservation acts that were intended to help elephants, tigers, and rhinos in Africa and Asia.

The Great Ape Conservation Fund allows the U.S. Fish and Wildlife Service to give grants to researchers. These researchers intend to help preserve habitats, enforce laws against poaching, and promote education about the animals. In 2005, $1.4 million was given to help fund thirty projects that helped preserve great apes.

◄ A GROUP OF RWANDAN SCHOOL CHILDREN LEARN ABOUT THE IMPORTANCE OF PROTECTING GORILLAS.

Gorillas Inspire International Cooperation

According to the International Union for Conservation of Nature (IUCN): "National and international laws controlling hunting or capture of gorillas exist in all habitat countries, but enforcement . . . is almost non-existent."[6]

In 2007, ten central African countries signed a treaty agreeing to work for gorilla conservation. The countries agreed to do several specific actions, such as maintaining gorillas' habitats.

▼ GORILLAS MAY BE BETTER PROTECTED IN THE FUTURE.

▲ CREATIVE FUND-RAISING HELPS BONOBOS AND OTHER GREAT APES.

REASON TO CARE # 48

Groups and Companies Raise Money for Great Apes

Many groups have found creative ways to help support great apes. For example, Ape Conservation Effort, a group based in Atlanta, Georgia, conducts fund-raising activities to help support great apes. An event called Apes in the Arts is a silent auction featuring artwork by gorillas and orangutans. Nature's Path, a company that produces organic foods, sells a cereal named Gorilla Munch. One percent of the sales of the cereal are donated to help conserve wildlife, including great apes.

Some People Fight for Apes' Rights

Some organizations, such as the Great Ape Project, want to have the great apes declared as persons by the United Nations. This would give great apes basic human rights, including the right to life, to freedom, and not to be tortured. Researcher Jane Goodall points out that chimpanzees can still be legally bought and sold. Declaring them persons would mean no one could own a great ape; they would have the right to freedom.

Other people point out that humans have rights, but also responsibilities. They are responsible for following laws. A great ape could not be expected to keep responsibilities and therefore should not be given rights, they argue. However, human rights are granted to children, who are not expected to live up to certain responsibilities. Organizations continue to debate the issue.

► SOME ORGANIZATIONS BELIEVE THAT APES SHOULD BE GIVEN HUMAN RIGHTS.

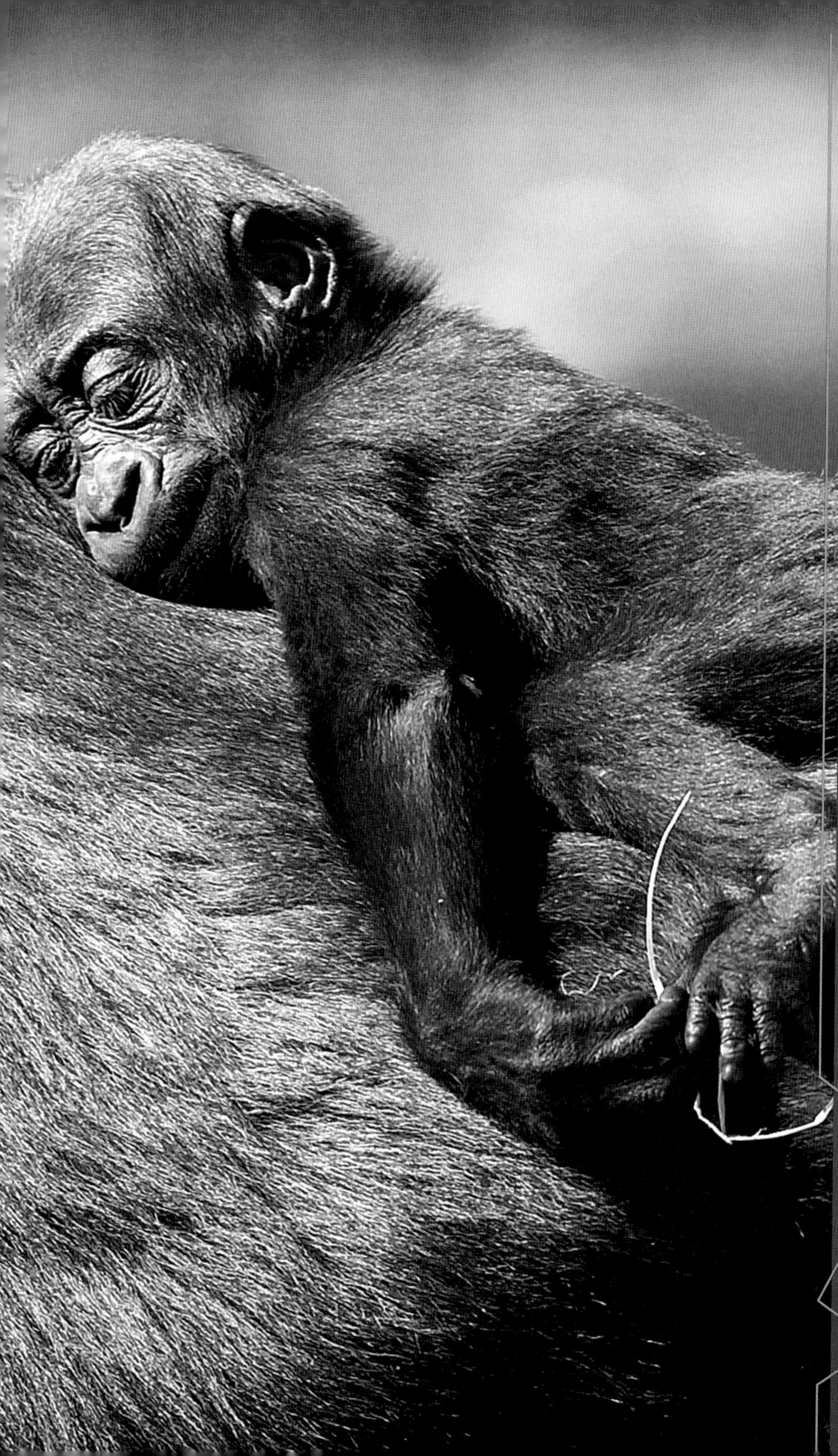

You Can Help Save Great Apes

Fun and Rewarding Ways to Help Save Great Apes

- Contact organizations that are dedicated to the conservation of great apes. They can provide educational materials and ways for you to help.
- Watch a documentary about great apes.
- Write to advertisers and television companies that portray great apes in a way that does not show how endangered they are.
- Check with your local zoo to find out if it is involved in any programs to help great apes. Maybe you can get involved!
- Tell your parents to avoid buying tropical woods for flooring and furniture. The Forestry Stewardship Council puts its label on wood that is cut without harming forests. Saving ape habitats is a critical part of saving apes.
- Write an e-mail to the editor of your local newspaper to let others know about the dangers to great apes.

▶ YOU CAN HELP SAVE GREAT APES!

GLOSSARY

adapt—To change to meet the demands of the environment.

bushmeat—Meat eaten by humans that comes from wild animals hunted in the tropical forest.

canopy—The layer of a forest made up of the tops of trees.

captivity—Being in the zoo instead of the wild.

conservation—The protection of nature and animals.

deforestation—The destruction of a forest by cutting down trees, by burning, or both.

endangered—At risk of becoming extinct.

environment—The natural world; the area in which a person or animal lives.

extinct—Died out completely.

family—A group of related animals.

grooming—A practice primates do to clean each other and express friendship.

habitat—The place in which an animal lives; the features of that place including plants, landforms, and weather.

Hominidae—The family of primates that once included only one living species, Homo sapiens, but now includes all of the great apes in most classifications.

order—A category of similar families, or groups, of animals.

palm oil—An edible butter-like substance derived from African palm trees.

parasite—An organism that lives on a plant or animal of another species and benefits from that host.

population—The total number of a group of animals.

rain forest—A forest that experiences 80 to 400 inches of rainfall per year; rain forests also have a high number of different species.

rehabilitation—The act of restoring a person or an animal back to health or normal life.

species—A specific group of animals with shared physical characteristics and genes; members within a species can breed with each other to produce offspring.

subspecies—A group within a species that is different from other groups in that species.

territory—An area defended by one animal against others.

virus—A microscopic agent that spreads disease.

FURTHER READING

Books

Fleisher, Paul. *Gorillas*. Tarrytown, NY: Benchmark Books, 2001.

Goldish, Meish. *Orangutans*. New York: Bearport, 2008.

Kalman, Bobbie, and Hadley Dyer. *Endangered Chimpanzees*. New York: Crabtree, 2005.

Roe-Pimm, Nancy. *The Heart of the Beast: Eight Great Gorilla Stories*. Plain City, OH: Darby Creek Publishing, 2007.

Taylor, Barbara. *Apes and Monkeys*. Boston, MA: Kingfisher, 2004.

Turner, Pamela S. *Gorilla Doctors: Saving Endangered Great Apes*. New York: Houghton Mifflin, 2008.

Internet Addresses

African Wildlife Foundation—Bonobos
<http://www.awf.org/content/general/detail/3495>

Ape Alliance
<http://www.4apes.com>

The Jane Goodall Institute
<http://www.janegoodall.org/>

SOURCE NOTES

Source Notes

1. Michael Leach, *The Great Apes: Our Face in Nature's Mirror* (London: Blandford, 1996), p. 66.

2. Paolo Cavalieri and Peter Singer, eds, *The Great Ape Project: Equality Beyond Humanity* (New York: St. Martin's Griffin, 1994), p. 44.

3. Michael Leach, *The Great Apes: Our Face in Nature's Mirror* (London: Blandford, 1996), p. 66.

4. "Lincoln Park Zoo study reveals that inappropriate media portrayal of chimpanzees may hinder conservation efforts," *Lincoln Park Zoo*, March 13, 2008. <http://www.lpzoo.org/info/media-center/main/031308_Chimpanzees_portrayal_general_post_embargo_release.pdf> (April 10, 2009).

5. Christian Nellemann, et al. (eds), "The Last Stand of the Orangutan," *United Nations Environment Programme*, 2007, <http://www.unep-wcmc.org/resources/publications/LastStand.htm> (Sept. 11, 2008).

6. P. D. Walsh, et al., "Gorilla Gorilla," *International Union for Conservation of Nature, 2007 IUCN Red List of Threatened Species*, <www.iucnredlist.org> (July 3, 2008).

INDEX